AF504443

A GIFT

just for you

To:

From:

Copyright © Katy A Lauren 2021

ALL RIGHTS RESERVED

No part of this publication may be reproduced, distributed, or transmitted in any form or by any means, including photocopying, recording, or other electronic or mechanical methods, without the prior written permission of the author/publisher.

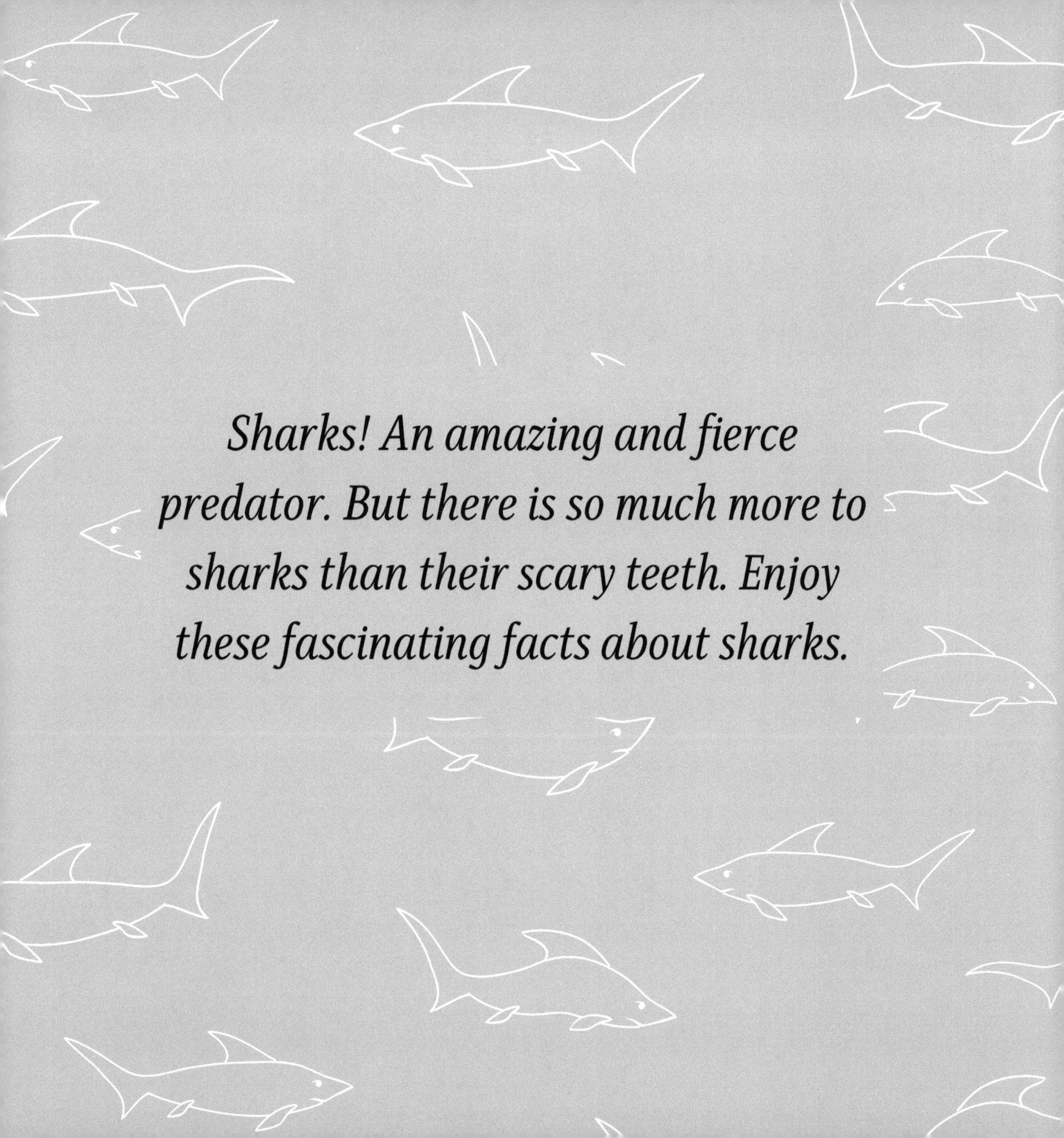

Sharks! An amazing and fierce predator. But there is so much more to sharks than their scary teeth. Enjoy these fascinating facts about sharks.

Did you know that Great White Sharks can go weeks without eating?

Did you know that Hammerhead Sharks can see all around themselves? They have a 360-degree field of vision.

Did you know that some shark species lay eggs and others give birth to live young? The Port Jackson Shark even carries the eggs around in her mouth until she finds a safe spot to place them.

Did you know that sharks don't have any bones? They have flexible cartilage. It's the reason they can open their mouths this wide.

Did you know that the world's largest shark is the Whale Shark and it only eats tiny ocean plankton? It can also live up to 150 years.

Did you know that the Greenland Shark can live over 400 years and is the slowest shark on earth? They move at an average of 0.8 mph and live in waters where the temperature is 30 to 50°F.

Did you know that sharks never run out of teeth? They have several rows of teeth that will push forward anytime a tooth is lost. During a shark's lifetime it can produce over 30,000 teeth.

Did you know that not all sharks live in the ocean? Some sharks can live in salt water or fresh water.

Did you know that sharks get scared? Even the fiercest shark has been known to avoid places where Killer Whales feed.

Did you know that some shark moms can be pregnant for up to two years?

Did you know that most sharks can see well in daylight waters and have excellent night vision?

Did you know that a shark's skin feels like sandpaper? This is because their skin is made of small teeth-like structures called placoid scales.

Did you know that Basking Sharks are filter feeders? They open their jaws up wide to gather tiny zooplankton and small fish and then filter out the water.

Did you know that sharks have excellent hearing? They can hear low-frequency signals and their ears are on either side of their head, behind their eyes.

Did you know that sharks have lived on earth for over 455 million years?

Did you know that scientists guess the age of a shark based on the number of rings on its vertebrae?

Did you know that not all sharks have the same shape of teeth? Some sharks have long, pointed teeth others have triangle shaped teeth.

Did you know that there are over 500 species of sharks? But don't worry most are not dangerous to humans.

www.ingramcontent.com/pod-product-compliance
Lightning Source LLC
Chambersburg PA
CBHW042008110726
48006CB00004B/1011